1968

RUSSIAN ICONS

SPRING ART BOOKS

RUSSIAN ICONS

by Tamara Talbot Rice

SPRING BOOKS • LONDON

I must express my sincere thanks to Mr George R. Hann and to Mr S. G. Gasilov for providing the bulk of the illustrations for this book. But for their help the necessary colour plates could not have been obtained, and it would have proved impossible to acquaint Western art-lovers with the fine examples of Russian medieval painting assembled in this volume. I am especially grateful to the USSR Academy of Fine Arts for the use of their photographs for Plates 2 — 6, 9 — 15, 24, 25, 40, and 47. The Virgin of Vladimir (Plate 1) is reproduced by courtesy of the Tretyakov Gallery.

First published 1963
2nd impression (revised) 1964

Published by
SPRING BOOKS
Westbook House • Fulham Broadway • London
© Paul Hamlyn Limited 1963
Printed in Czechoslovakia by Svoboda, Prague
T 1446

Contents

Introduction

The element of precision inherent in facts tends, by its very nature, to obliterate variations and complexities, and it is thus often inclined to distort our viewing of the past. A case in point is the prevailing tendency to think of western Europe as a wholly Christian entity from, at any rate, as far back as the sixth century A.D. In actual fact, even as late as the ninth century — at the very time when certain Varangian princes were penetrating into what is known today as western Russia, in order to gain control of the region's great waterways — much of Scandinavia was still pagan, as were large areas of such basically Christian countries as Ireland* and even many a backwater of rural England, though supposedly converted. Seen in this perspective, Russia's conversion at the very end of the tenth century does not appear nearly so tardy an event, when it is considered factually, as when seen against the background provided by such countries as Byzantium, Armenia and Georgia, which had been Christian since the third or fourth century.

Several churches existed in Kiev for a number of years prior to the principality's conversion to Christianity, but they were intended primarily for the use of the foreign merchants who had begun to flock to this flourishing commercial centre in ever-increasing numbers. The bulk of the local population remained pagan, worshipping idols of various sorts until the year 988, when Vladimir, reigning great prince of Kiev, having himself recently become a convert, decreed that his people were to follow his example and accept baptism in mass. His wishes were carried out with characteristic Russian thoroughness and determination; universal baptism was applied, the innumerable idols to whom the people had turned for hope and comfort were ruthlessly destroyed, and Kiev, the kernel from which present-day Russia has developed, was rapidly provided with the churches necessary for the new cult. The foundation stone of its first large, and for some forty years, principal church, that

* W. E. D. Allen, *The Poet and the Spae-Wife*, Dublin and London, 1960, pp. 40—41

7

of the Virgin of the Dime, was laid by Vladimir in 991. This building's importance was outstripped in 1036 or 1037, when Yaroslav, Vladimir's youngest son and successor, founded the cathedral of Hagia Sophia. Though the latter was neither capable of eclipsing, nor was it ever intended that it should eclipse the magnificence of Constantinople's cathedral of the same name, it is a superb building, and it can hold its own with the foremost Western cathedrals of similar date. It set the seal on Kiev's splendour no less than on its piety, both of which came as a surprise to Western visitors. Dittmar, bishop of Megibur (976 — 1018) was astonished to find 400 churches standing within Kiev's walls. Some of these were doubtless of modest dimensions and constructed of wood, the local building material in the area. Others strove to emulate the grandeur of the cathedral church of the Virgin of the Dime, but the two which were destined to rank with Hagia Sophia, the church of St Michael and the cathedral church of the Monastery of the Caves, were not built until 1070 and 1073 respectively.

Kiev was not the only Russian stronghold of Christianity; other thriving urban centres, cities such as Novgorod, for example, and its satellite Pskov, Yaroslavl and the principality of Vladimir-Suzdal were as fervent as Kiev in their faith and scarcely less well endowed with churches, many of which were as lovely and as ornate as the majority of those in Kiev. Nevertheless, some traces of paganism persisted here and there in the remoter, thickly wooded regions of northern Russia, even though the country as a whole had become a basically devout and genuinely Christian state. The speed with which Christianity had made itself supreme in the land was not entirely due to the energetic measures which Vladimir and his immediate followers had taken to enforce its acceptance. The new doctrine had appealed to all that was best in the people, and the magnificent setting provided by the Greek Orthodox church, satisfying as it did their innate love of splendour and of grave beauty, played its part in attaching them to the new creed. The greatly revered paintings which adorned the inner walls of their churches helped to further the cause by providing worshippers with an inexhaustible fund from which to draw material to occupy their lively and active imaginations. It was, however, the icons that won the peoples' hearts, riveting their attention, and serving as both the focus and the source of inspiration of their devotions.

The mural decorations inside the churches, which were concerned with recording the story of the scriptures and providing visual representations of the persons who figure in them, had a somewhat remote and aloof air because of their height on the walls and the distance which separated them from the worshippers. They had none of the intimacy which the Russians required as an accompaniment to their faith.

The scenes and figures in the paintings seemed as far removed from them as heaven itself, and the people were left desiring something more accessible and compassionate. This they found in the individual figures and scenes which were reproduced on the portable panels we know as icons. In Russia, these panels provided the answer to a deeply felt spiritual need, with the result that, whereas mosaics can perhaps be regarded as the supreme form of religious art of Byzantium, and wall paintings as the finest achievement of the artists of the Balkan world, icons were destined to inspire the Russians to produce their finest pictorial works, and in the process, to create a school of painting which is just as significant, and aesthetically no less interesting and satisfying than the far better known pictures left to us by the primitive painters of Italy.

To begin with, in Russia, few icons, and very often no more than one, were attached to the screen which, in the earlier churches, separated the nave from the sanctuary. Since these generally depicted holy or saintly personages — often a local saint — or the religious scene after which the church was named, such icons soon became known as *mestniya* or 'place' icons. However, by the fourteenth century the fondness for icons resulted in so many panels being fixed to the screen that it led to the invention and widespread use of the iconostasis — a combined altar screen and icon stand — filling the entire width of the church and reaching upward to a quite considerable height. The iconostasis was made of wood, which was generally elaborately carved and painted, often even gilt. The icons were arranged in it in tiers, in a carefully prescribed order. In accordance with this there were two doors at its centre, known as the Royal Doors because they gave access to the altar. It was customary for these doors to be decorated with renderings of the evangelists, though occasionally local saints were depicted instead, and also with paintings representing the Annunciation and the Eucharist. The 'place' icons were ranged along either side of the Royal Doors, thus completing the first row or 'tier', as it is called, of the iconostasis. Set immediately above the Royal Doors were the icons forming the Deesis group, consisting of Christ in the centre with the Virgin on His right and St John on His left, interceding with Him for mankind. The Deesis icons, and consequently also all the others in that tier, were often larger in size than the others, and although they were generally shown on three separate panels, they are also sometimes found on a large single one. On either side of the Deesis group stretched icons representing the archangels and the fathers of the church. The third tier of the iconostasis was concerned with illustrating the church's Twelve Festivals, that is to say, the Annunciation, the Nativity, the Presentation of Christ or the Purification of the Virgin, the

Baptism, the Raising of Lazarus, the Transfiguration, the Entry to Jerusalem, the Crucifixion, the Resurrection, the Ascension, the Pentecost and the Assumption of the Virgin. The fourth tier displayed the Virgin in the centre with the prophets of the Old Testament, generally headed by David and Solomon, standing on either side of her. When space permitted the inclusion of a fifth tier, it contained at its centre the pictorial rendering of the mystical theme of the 'Lord God Sabaoth', symbolising the Trinity, often also called 'Paternity', because it displays renderings of the Father, Son and Holy Ghost. The space on either side of that icon was filled in with panels displaying the patriarchs of the Old Testament. In addition to the icons belonging to the iconostasis, it was customary also to place single icons in the body of the church, and it was likewise the practice for an icon with a taper burning before it to be set up in private dwellings, occupying the inner right-hand corner of a room, where the religious picture helped to keep the spirit of Christianity alive in the home.

Though icons were believed to act as intercessors and were sometimes also invested with miraculous powers, they were never confused with or treated as idols; rather it was felt that the subject matter, because of its divinity and saintliness, somehow contrived to transmit a particle of the goodness inherent in its themes to its pictorial representations. It was also held that the intrinsic holiness of the subject matter demanded, if the painting were to prove satisfying and potent, that the artist responsible for its creation should be as righteous and devout a person as possible. It was because of this belief that most of the medieval painters were monks, and that, in later times, the occupation passed from father to son, the painters endeavouring to regulate their lives in accordance with the Bible's precepts, in much the same way that participants in the Oberammergau Passion play strive to make their daily behaviour conform to that of the divine or saintly beings whose lives they re-enact once each decade.

When an icon attained to a startling degree of beauty, spirituality and emotion, it often seemed to the worshippers that some element other than the merely human had helped to fashion such a painting; in other words, it was often the pictures of most outstanding artistic merit that were credited with miraculous powers. And is there not, after all, something divine and marvellous, something perhaps not wholly terrestial, about a work of art which retains throughout the centuries its appeal and its power to move, with the result that successive generations continue readily to accept it as a masterpiece?

Although miracle-working icons were objects of particular veneration, their number was exceedingly small; nor were they ever mistaken for the ultimate purpose of prayer. In this respect, the rôle of an icon is similar to that of a religious painting in the Roman Catholic world, and it does not differ very much in style from the paintings produced by the Italian primitives, for both types of illustrations stem from the same Byzantine and early Christian sources. However, whereas under the impact of the Renaissance, the Roman Catholic painters of religious subjects were permitted to develop their individuality, to experiment in composition and to adopt a naturalistic style, under the rigid control of the Orthodox hierarchy icon painters were obliged to adhere to the iconography and style which had been evolved by their earliest forerunners. The necessity of retaining a predetermined form and style did not, however, have a stultifying effect upon Orthodox artists of medieval times; rather did it help them to concentrate on the ideas underlying this form. It is the measure in which each of the medieval artists succeeded in endowing his paintings with an inner fire that, to a great extent, established the artistic quality of an icon.

It was part of the iconographic convention that the personages represented by the painters were to retain the contours of ordinary human beings. It was at the same time essential for those who were of holy origin to be so obviously invested with celestial characteristics that all who saw them should at once be able to realise that these figures stood apart even from the saints, prophets and fathers of the church; but these latter personages had in their turn to be marked by an asceticism which distinguished them from their fellow men. It was thus, on the one hand, imperative that all the figures shown on icons should appear human, but at the same time it was equally necessary that none should ever be mistaken for an ordinary human being. Furthermore, each one had to be endowed with the distinctive features which would, throughout the centuries, enable each personage to be recognised at a glance in every section of the Orthodox world; where even a child should know instantly whether he is gazing upon the features, say, of a St Nicholas or a St Paul. These dual requirements, the realistic and the metaphysical, had to be exactly balanced and blended if icons were to be successful in fulfilling their prime duty — that of inspiring both the illiterate and the cultivated worshippers.

The technique of painting in tempera upon panels was a very old one, stemming from the tomb portraits of ancient Egypt. The iconography imposed upon Byzantine painters had been evolved by the Eastern church in early Christian times, and was so closely adhered to by all branches of the Orthodox church that even in the flat grass lands and densely wooded areas of western Russia, where torrents gushing from clefts in towering mountains were as unknown as the bright and varied colours which invest the scenery of the Middle East with its peculiarly arresting quality, these alien elements were retained, and not only accepted in such scenes as those of the Baptism or the Nativity, but even considered as natural and topographically convincing.

The iconography, style and conventions of the religious art of the East Christian church were fully developed and firmly established in Byzantium long before the time of Russia's conversion to Christianity, so that when Vladimir looked to Byzantium for the churches and the church furnishings which he needed for his newly baptised people, he naturally enough acquired from Constantinople a fully formed style in both art and architecture. This style proved sympathetic to the Russians, and as a result they were able to assimilate it quickly, to express themselves freely in its idiom and, before long, to start laying the foundations of a national and essentially Russian school of painting within the Byzantine framework.

To the newcomer from the Western world, all icons tend at first to look alike, yet in reality no two are identical. Anyone who is prepared to devote a little time to their contemplation, stilling his mind and letting his spirit commune with the picture while his eyes study its contours, will very soon learn to recognise an icon of quality, and to distinguish between one produced by a Byzantine or later Greek artist and one painted by a Slav, whether Serbian, Bulgarian or Russian; the difference between a Cypriot or Venetian panel will likewise become as clearly apparent as that which sets a Cappadocian or Anatolian icon in distinct groups. Greater application is necessary in order to date an icon or to recognise the styles which pertain to the various schools within these major groups. Russian art is particularly rich in the number and quality of its regional schools. Broadly speaking, the majority of its finest icons stem from Kiev, Novgorod, Pskov, the Vladimir-Suzdal area, Yaroslavl and Moscow, but many a minor centre, such as Riazan, Chernigov, Polotsk, Galich, Vladimir-Volynsk and Tver, to name but some of those that boasted schools of their own, produced work of very high quality. Each was responsible for paintings which deserve to rank with Europe's great masterpieces, and it is now but a question of time before their importance becomes universally recognised.

The earliest icons and mural decorations on Russian soil were produced in Kiev by Greek artists, the best of whom were employed on decorating the Church of the Dime, the cathedral of Hagia Sophia, the church of St Michael and the cathedral church of the Monastery of the Caves. The decorations in Hagia Sophia survive in part to bear testimony to the high standard achieved and to indicate the closeness of the artistic links binding Kiev to Constantinople. Yet even in these early works Russian characteristics intrude in the form of more naturalistic poses, less severe faces, stockier bodies and a more linear outline, making it clear that Russians were from the start working with the Greeks, though it is probable that in the opening phase they did so in the capacity of assistants. With the establishment of the famous Monastery of the Caves, Bulgarian influences were introduced into Kiev as a result of the close contacts which the monastery formed with the monastic communities on Mount Athos and, more especially, with the Balkan foundations there. The Monastery of the Caves also fostered the growth of Russian nationalism, and it was within its walls that the first Russian painter to have his name mentioned in a chronicle, the artist Alimpy, was trained. The monastery probably possessed its own icon painting workshop, the members of which were doubtless instructed by the Greek artists who had been employed on decorating its cathedral. Other workshops for the production of icons must have existed in the town itself and possibly also in the sovereign's palace, and it is unfortunate that no icons of eleventh-century date and of Kievian workmanship have as yet been discovered. However, quite a number of twelfth- and thirteenth-century panels survive, many of them in good condition: they include the fine twelfth-century icon of St George in the Cathedral of the Assumption, Moscow, and an icon of the Virgin of Svensk, preserved in the Tretyakov Gallery in Moscow, which has often been ascribed to Alimpy. Soviet scholars now regard it as a later work, but it may well be a copy of an earlier icon, and perhaps of the one painted by this master, for master he must have been to have had his name perpetuated by his contemporaries. The prototype for the surviving icon must have belonged to Alimpy's monastery, since the iconography of the Virgin, showing her holding the Child in the act of performing a blessing, is of the type which is associated with the Monastery of the Caves. On the surviving panel, the Virgin and Child are flanked by two priests painted in an archaic, though realistic, style who represent the founders of the monastery.

Some of the earliest and assuredly among the loveliest of surviving Russian icons were produced in the Vladimir-Suzdal principality, prior to the Mongol domination of Russia (1242). It was in the twelfth century, when the principality's links with Kiev were extremely close, that Vladimir Monomachus, great prince of Kiev, presented the town of Rostov with an icon which had been painted by Alimpy. It was then, too, that the famous icon of the Virgin of Vladimir (Plate 1), which was imported to Kiev from Byzantium prior to 1155, was seized by Prince Andrew Bogolyubski in 1164 when he broke loose from the suzerainty of his father and liege lord, and transported by him to his own capital of Vladimir. It is idle to speculate on the appearance of Alimpy's icon, but the extent of the influence which the icon of the Virgin of Vladimir exercised on the artists of the Vladimir-Suzdal area, and through them of Russia as a whole, is clearly to be seen in their works. The icons of the Vladimir-Suzdalian school are impregnated with the humanism which distinguishes the icon of the Virgin of Vladimir from all other known Byzantine paintings — a humanism that was perhaps especially introduced into it at the request of a Russian patron. In addition to this humanism, the Vladimir-Suzdalian icons have a lyrical quality which is wholly Russian, and also an elegant sophistication for which the Georgian wife of Prince Andrew's son may have been in part responsible. Notwithstanding their gentleness, there is nothing sentimental about these icons; their dignity and grace is as assured and satisfying as that which distinguishes the lovely and exceptionally ornate stone churches built in the towns of the principality at the same date. The influence of the icons is clearly to the fore in the panels which were produced in Yaroslavl in the early thirteenth century, but in the latter, the delicacy and elegance of the Suzdalian style are sharpened by a greater severity of conception and a more monumental manner of presentation.

The Yaroslavl school of painting proved both creative and enduring. Springing up late in the twelfth century, its artists tempered the forceful yet compassionate demeanour of their figures by an elaborate treatment of their draperies and the inclusion of numerous decorative details. By the seventeenth century, when Yaroslavl had grown into an important centre for the production of pottery, more especially of glazed tiles, her painters had evolved an enchanting, decorative genre style which survived in folk art down to the revolution, and which still persists in the scenes which adorn the papier mâché boxes that are being produced today in the USSR.

Magnificent though these early icons are, they are too few in quantity to give an idea of the general standard which had been attained by the painters of the pre-Mongol period, and it is for this reason that the icons which were produced in great numbers between the thirteenth and the sixteenth centuries in cities which were never occupied by the Mongols, especially in Novgorod and its satellite city of Pskov, have come to rank as the chief glory of Russian medieval art. In them all the various national elements which had appeared sporadically in other areas were assembled, blended and developed into a vital and flourishing art. The graphic approach which still characterises what is best in Russian painting, the delicate yet assured, elegant yet forthright line, the love and feeling for glowing yet thoroughly harmonious colours, the deeply mystical conception expressed naturally but with profound conviction — all these elements appear in Novgorodian icons, fused into an inspired and admirably blended entity. Unlike his Western fellow-artists, none of the Orthodox painters of this period, not even the greatest among them, was ever troubled by a desire to express his own individuality or to give reign to his imagination. At this period, each was wholly concerned in manifesting in his work the religious fervour which served as the mainspring

14

of his life, striving to demonstrate his faith with such radiance that its incandescence might succeed in kindling a like devotion in those who gazed upon his paintings.

Until the seventeenth century, when the impact of the Western world began to make itself felt in Moscow, none of these artists attempted to alter the iconographic tradition imposed upon him by the church, nor thought of experimenting with technical innovations, such as those concerning true perspective. This should not be taken to mean that these painters failed to take an interest in the technical aspects of pictorial composition — even a cursory glance at an icon will show that it followed its own rules of perspective, that problems of spacing and presentation were considered, that, in each, the proportions were cleverly worked out and the scenes combined and arranged to produce a balanced, rhythmical and uncrowded effect, while the able use of colours and lines contrived skilfully to direct the eye to the icon's focal point. So absorbed were the icon painters in their calling and their faith that each was content to work anonymously. All shared the outlook which Ananda Coomaraswamy has discussed in *Christian and Oriental Philosophy of Art**, explaining that 'the anonymity of the artist belongs to a type of culture dominated by the longing to be liberated from oneself. All the force of this philosophy is directed against the delusion "I am the doer". "I" am not in fact the doer, but the instrument; human individuality is not an end but only a means. The supreme achievement of individual consciousness is to lose or find (both words mean the same) itself in what is both its first beginning and its last end.'

From the time of Russia's conversion, Novgorod had vied with Kiev in the intensity of its religious fervour, in the keenness of its national consciousness and in the vigour with which it gave rein to its commercial pursuits. Novgorod's Hagia Sophia was as old, as large and, although devoid of mosaic decorations, scarcely less splendid than Kiev's. Like Kiev, Novgorod, too, found the basic inspiration for its religious art in Byzantium, and from as early as the twelfth century icons of superb quality were being produced within its territory. One of the earliest and most venerated of these icons displays the Vernicle; it is now preserved in the Tretyakov Gallery in Moscow. It is a large double-sided processional icon, and its antiquity is attested to by an illumination in a manuscript in the Historical Museum at Moscow, dated to 1262 (Khlud. 187, 1), in which it figures. The face of the icon, that is to say the side showing the Vernicle, is strongly Byzantine in character. The Saviour is shown with His hair parted in the centre in neat coils picked out in gold. The reverse displays the Adoration of the Dead Christ; it is painted by a different hand and in a far more Russian manner than the Vernicle. This icon is one of the remarkable group which includes

* Dover Publications, N. Y., 1956

the famous icon of the Golden-haired Virgin, and which Professor Lazarev is inclined to ascribe to a court workshop. The entire group clearly demonstrates the closeness of Novgorod's artistic links with Byzantium, for in each of these icons the elongated faces and intense expressions of the Constantinopolitan style recur; yet there also appears in them the innate Russian liking for bright yet delicate colours, the fondness for attractive decorative effects and the striving towards an almost silhouette-like outline. With the passing years, the Novgorodians softened the severity of these Byzantinesque faces, and by the fourteenth century less austere, though equally intense renderings had been evolved. There was then a preference for showing them against a vivid red background, but somewhat later the white or, rather, pale ochre backgrounds which characterise the Novgorodian school were introduced, and then the painting was executed in a rather freer manner.

The Mongol conquest of Russia stopped short of Novgorod, so that life in the merchant republic was able to flow along normal lines; and whereas in the occupied areas artists were obliged to mark time, those working in Novgorodian territory were able to develop freely. As a result, the Novgorodian style had crystallised by the fourteenth century; it was a simpler style than the Byzantine, more linear, clearer in colour and, at any rate at first, distinguished by fewer highlights. It underwent no marked change throughout the first half of the century, but in the 1370's, there arrived in Novgorod a Constantinopolitan painter — he may well have come there as a refugee — who became known throughout Russia by the name of Theophanes the Greek. Like his countryman El Greco, he was proud of his origin, yet he became as much a Russian painter as Theotocopoulos a Spanish one, for it was in Russia that Theophanes developed into one of Europe's greatest religious painters. His Russian contemporary, the chronicler Epiphanius, recorded that in 1413, when Theophanes was living in Moscow and had become an old man, he was venerated in the capital not only as an artist but also as a sage and a philosopher. When engaged on mural paintings, Theophanes used to astonish Russian onlookers by his skill in working free hand, without the aid of sketches or outlines. In his murals, his saints are strongly Byzantine in character — severe and austere figures who had known and overcome temptation; his colours are a blend of sombre Byzantine tones, with a predominance of mauves and greys, but enlivened with touches of the particularly Russian shades of yellow, pink and green, and a considerable use of white; his brush stroke is incisive and passionate, rendered fluid by the extensive use of highlights.

The iconostasis is the focal point in a Russian church interior. As such, it attracts immediate attention, and the numerous icons set in it are seen as a whole and at a glance. Great skill and restraint are essential in order to avoid creating an impression of confusion and of overcrowding. In Byzantium Theophanes had probably not been used to producing icons intended to be seen in these conditions, but in Novgorod the demand for icons required for use in iconostases was so great that Theophanes must have applied himself to mastering the problems arising from the interrelationship of a considerable number of paintings which were to be seen in close juxtaposition. In the very few icons which are ascribed to him, he seems to have assimilated a number of Novgorodian influences which do not appear in his mural paintings. Thus, the icons in the Deesis tier of the iconostasis in the Cathedral of the Annunciation in Moscow's Kremlin, notably those representing the archangel Gabriel, St Peter, St Basil the Great, and St John the Evangelist, all of which Soviet scholars consider to be by Theophanes, display the simplicity which is essential to the icons of an iconostasis, but in order to intensify the ethereality of his figures, the Greek artist elongated the already tall Novgorodian silhouette; however, he continued to apply his paint in the sweeping strokes which distinguish the mural artist from the icon painter.

Theophanes's influence on the painters of Novgorod was as great as that which he was later to exercise over the artists working in Moscow, but before discussing the rôle which he played in the capital and outlining the rise of the Muscovite school of painting, it is desirable to digress a little in order to devote some attention to certain of the local schools which sprang up under Novgorodian influence, doing so before the artists of Novgorod were themselves overshadowed by the products of Moscow's workshops. These provincial schools absorbed many of the features which the Novgorodian had developed in the course of the thirteenth and fourteenth centuries, notably a fondness for firm yet sinuous lines, culminating in the rounded, gently sloping shoulders of their figures, a mastery at combining luminous and very varied colours, in which red and gold predominated, with much white, emerald green, the peculiarly Russian shades of pink and yellow, and several tones of blue. In addition, Pskov displayed a preference for dark green backgrounds, but other regions experimented with even darker ones, combining them with borders of orange-red: later, most of the provincial schools adopted the Novgorodian habit of using numerous highlights, but the northern schools inclined towards more angular outlines than the Novgorodian, often stressing the horizontal elements in their compositions. Saints presented in rows, with emblems decorating their vestments, became popular; they were given the sturdy bodies and round heads of the Russians, the burning eyes peculiar to mystics and the long, ascetic nose which is rarely seen in Russia but which Byzantine paintings had rendered familiar there. In Pskov, the local style was a strongly personal one: at first rather archaic, it later came to include the profuse use of darkish highlights and much fleck-ing. Icons from the remoter regions are often a trifle naive, but in the more sophisti-cated works, this naiveté expressed itself in a love of imagery and enchanting decoration which is characteristic of Russian folk art. This tendency is most noticeable in the small scenes framing the centrally placed figure of a saint, illustrating the notable events of his life. Icons of this type are called *zhiteynie* or 'biographical'; they became extremely popular in the fifteenth century in many districts, but the folklorist element is most marked in those which were produced at that time in Vologda. The inspiration for this folklorist element may well have been aroused first in Novgorod, when the city began to sense the danger which Moscow was so soon to present to its indepen-dence; for the tendency is seen expressed at its best in a remarkable early fifteenth-century Novgorodian icon, several versions of which exist, depicting the battle be-tween the Novgorodians and the Suzdalians. It commemorates the protection afforded to Novgorod by the miraculous icon of the Virgin of the Sign *(Znamenie)* in 1169, when the city was attacked by the men of Suzdal; its scenes are rendered in an unusually realistic, remarkably decorative and basically folklorist manner.

From the twelfth to the fourteenth centuries, the least important of all the provincial schools were those of Moscow and of Tver, which were to some extent linked. At the time both cities were extremely small and insignificant, but even at this early date Moscow had already established artistic links with the principality of Vladimir-Suzdal, with the result that her artists were primarily affected by trends making themselves felt within the principality. These continued to stir the Muscovites in the fifteenth century, even after their ruler had insisted on many leading Novgorodian artists moving to Moscow to help to expand the latter school of painting, and over and again the metropolitan painters were encouraged to look to Vladimir-Suzdal for guidance.

Moscow's rise, both in the political and in the artistic spheres, dates from her victory over the Mongols at the battle of Kulikovo in 1380, when the Tartar hold over the country was so effectively weakened that the dream of Russian independence acquired considerable reality. For the first time for well over a century, the country's future seemed rich in promise, the outlook so encouraging, that Moscow's growth developed apace, and the Russians once again set out to strengthen their contacts with Con-stantinople. As a result, as early as 1385, a Greek artist was commissioned to paint an icon of the Virgin of Tikhvin for Prince Dimitri Donskoi, the victor at Kulikovo, and some time between 1387 and 1395, the important series of icons known today as the Vysotski Deesis tier was brought to Moscow from Constantinople. It was also towards the end of that century, according to Professor Lazarev, not later than the year 1395, that Theophanes the Greek took up residence in Moscow, abandoning Novgorod. By 1404, Theophanes was deeply involved in work in the Kremlin where he was adorning the walls of the Cathedral of the Annunciation. Employed there as his assistants were two Russians whose names the chroniclers of the period made a point of including in their records. They were monks from the Monastery of the Trinity at Zagorsk: the elder was the painter Prokhor of Gorodetz; the other his pupil, Andrei Rublev — the man who was destined to become Russia's greatest medieval painter. Theophanes did much to stimulate Rublev's development, broadening his outlook without spoiling his very individual approach to his art. Indeed, the impact made by the Greek is to be seen in many other notable paintings produced in Moscow at that time, but it was not the only one at work there. Professor Lazarev sees other influences in the paintings dating from the late fourteenth and fifteenth centuries, and these the Soviet scholar has ascribed to artists fleeing to Moscow from the Balkans in the face of the ever-growing peril engendered by the Turks. However, in the fifteenth century, the formative influence over Muscovite artists was that which their fellow-countryman, the monk Andrei Rublev, was to exercise over them. His gentle spirituality, his incisive yet softly flowing lines and his elimination of all unessentials became the criterion of beauty in the capital, setting the standard which most artists of the period strove to emulate.

Though Rublev is an artist who can hold his own beside any Western religious painter of the same period, Fra Angelico not excepted, exceedingly little is known about his life, and only a very small number of his works has survived. Since even the exact date of his birth is unknown, the Soviet authorities have associated it with the year 1360, but those scholars who incline to place it some ten years later may well be correct in their assumption. Rublev became a monk at the Monastery of the Trinity at Zagorsk in his youth and studied painting there under the monk Prokhor. His earliest known commissions took him to Zvenigorod in 1404. Three of the icons which he produced at this time — a Christ, an archangel Michael and an apostle Paul — still survive in the Tretyakov Gallery in Moscow, though they are in a very damaged condition. Even so, the marvellous harmony of their delicate yet sustained colours, their gentle yet unsentimental humanism and their sinuous yet firm lines endow these panels with a moving spirituality and an aesthetic quality that are outstanding. At some stage in his career Rublev worked in the Andronikov monastery; indeed, most of his life was spent in and around Moscow, where his name is recorded first in connection with the work which Theophanes, aided by Prokhor, was carrying out in the Cathedral of the Annunciation in 1405. Nevertheless, in 1408, Rublev was engaged on adorning the walls of the Cathedral of the Assumption at Vladimir. After that he appears to have returned to Moscow, probably to his own monastery at Zagorsk, and never again to have left it. There was much work for him to do there at the time, for many of its buildings had been heavily damaged in the course of a Tartar attack on the capital. It was there, probably in about 1411, that Rublev painted his masterpiece, the icon of the Old Testament Trinity, executing the panel in memory of the monastery's founder and first abbot, St Sergius of Radonezh, who had recently died. Rublev's closing years were devoted to painting the murals in the cathedral which had been built above St Sergius's tomb. He was assisted in this task by Danila Cherny, a painter of great distinction, with whom Rublev had for some years been running a joint workshop. The work occupied him until his death in about 1427.

Even though it was Rublev's influence which proved paramount throughout the fifteenth century, it was, nevertheless, under the impact of an artist called Dionysius that Muscovite painting attained to its fullest development. Dionysius must have been born within a decade or so of Rublev's death, that is to say in about 1440, for he is first mentioned in records as an assistant of the painter Mitrophanes, when the latter was engaged on decorating the Parfuntiev monastery, between 1467 and 1477. By 1484, however, Dionysius was himself being assisted by teams of icon painters, two of which included his sons. His death is placed sometime between the years 1502 and 1508.

Dionysius painted in an 'impressionist' manner; his figures are immensely elongated, and their heights appear even greater than they are because of the smallness of their heads, hands and feet. Furthermore, they are often presented poised on tiptoe or even slightly elevated from the ground, and this striving towards heaven, no less than the passionate character of the artist's brushwork, invests them with profound rapture. Dionysius's finest works are the murals of about 1500 which he executed for the Therapont monastery: very few icons by his own hand survive, but many biographical icons are traced to his workshop. These reflect the influence of Rublev no less than that of Theophanes, for the figures in them appear muted, stilled, as in Rublev's works, but they have Dionysius's elongated bodies and dreamily inclined heads. Though these icons are grand and forceful, some of them contain a faint element of effeminacy, which seems to foreshadow a period of decline. However, the colours remain as good as ever, Dionysius's very individual palette including various shades of pink, mauve, pale green and lemon yellow.

The typical fifteenth- and sixteenth-century Muscovite icons tended to be comparatively small in size, intimate and personal in style and subject, and decorative in appearance. Moscow had by then entered on a period of economic prosperity, and the easing of conditions brought into being a class of courtiers, soldiers and merchant princes who were in a position to build private chapels and to commission icons for use both in these chapels and their own homes. Personal icons — those representing the saints after whom their owners had been named — became popular. The foremost patrons of the day included the tsar and his relations, who looked for their needs to the artists employed in the royal workshops situated in the Palace of Arms, within the Kremlin's walls. Courtiers also placed their commissions with the metropolitan workshops, while enlightened merchant princes founded private workshops, which worked exclusively for them. The most famous and important of these private workshops was that which some members of the wealthy Stroganov family established in about 1580 on their country estate, situated in the district of Perm. It trained a surprisingly large number of artists of distinction and evolved a style of its own. Though it remained active until the 1620's, at its founder's death in 1601, many of its principal artists went to Moscow, where they quickly found employment in the royal workshops. There, they continued to work in their accustomed manner, influencing others to follow their example, until the style they practised came to be called Stroganov, in memory of the patrons who had inspired it. The artists themselves set out to perpetuate the association by frequently signing the reverse of their panels, adding after their names the appellation, 'Stroganov artist'.

The leading artists of the Stroganov school were Procopius Chirin, Simon Ushakov and four painters belonging to two generations of the Savin family, Istom, Theodore, Nazarius and Nicephorus. All six had been formed in the Stroganov workshop, where the best Novgorodian icons available were used to set the standard. Some of the artists, and these included Chirin, themselves hailed from Novgorod. On reaching Moscow these men, in their turn, set the standard and formed the taste of their patrons, but at the same time, if almost imperceptibly to begin with, they themselves came under the influence of the foreign artists who were by then living and working in Moscow. Through contact with these foreigners, the icon painters began taking an interest in realism, but the dogmatism of the clergy forbade them from indulging it, as it did their inclination towards self-expression and naturalism in art. Then the impact of the thriving commercial capital, in the life of which worldly considerations had begun to play an ever increasing part, started to affect the outlook of the Russian artists, disturbing their old ideas and undermining the ascetic spirit that was essential to the icon painters, so that the complex iconographic tradition ceased to satisfy them. On being forced to adhere to it, they discovered an outlet in the substitution of elaborate allegoric compositions containing numerous new, basically illustrative, elements and a profusion of decorative details in place of the simple themes which had sufficed their forbears. Subjects such as the 'Church Militant' and the 'Lord God Saboath' thus became extremely popular. Some of the Palace of Arms artists also tried their hands at portraiture of an iconic type, and genre scenes appeared in some religious mural works, notably at Yaroslavl. Nevertheless, the majority of the painters remained primarily icon painters. The most admired of their panels are those which are distinguished by a miniature technique of a kind intended to appeal primarily to the new class of art connoisseurs rather than to the whole-heartedly devout in outlook. Technically, notwithstanding a certain *fin-de-siècle* flavour, these paintings are excellent, comparable in conception to the small-sized Persian or Western miniatures of medieval date and, in their mass of minute detail, also to the subsidiary subject matter enlivening the large canvases of the Pre-Raphaelites. This preoccupation with incidentals was, however, an unhealthy sign; it led to a dead end — one from which the Western style of painting, introduced into Russia by Peter the Great, was unable to deflect it.

In the eighteenth century, under the impact of Peter's westernising policy, most artists of ability worked in the Western style. As a result, icon painting declined into a craft which was largely relegated to monks and hereditary artisans. Subsequent painters, working singly or in teams, continued to turn out large numbers of icons until the anti-religious measures introduced by the Soviet authorities early in the revolution put an end to their occupation. Most of the icons which were produced in the course of the late eighteenth and nineteenth centuries are little more than uninspired exercises in a style which had become moribund, for although a touch of real talent and true feeling occasionally ennobled some of these late panels, the majority remained fixed in an ancient form, to which a new, jejune sentimentality and a distressing touch of naturalism had been added, often destroying the grandeur of even the original conception. Thus, the art which had sprung into being in early Christian times in Byzantium died in Russia in the course of the early eighteenth century rather than in the twentieth. Throughout its long existence it had inspired the production of some superb masterpieces and of numerous works of outstanding merit. The appeal of these paintings is likely to endure for all time, but it should arouse an especially warm response today because, as in the case of contemporary painting, so too in that of the iconic type, the underlying thoughts and emotions are as important as the care and skill devoted to the choice of forms and colours, by means of which the latent sentiments and ideas are expressed.

The Technique of Icon Painting

The word 'icon' is a Greek one meaning image or reflection, and it was in that sense that it was applied to the portative representations of holy personages, saints or scenes taken from the scriptures. In 1650, when the schism which undermined the unity and power of the Russian church resulted in the destruction of a large number of icons, it was found easier to meet the heavy demand for replacements by producing metal moulds from which bronze or brass examples could be cast quickly. These variants were likewise referred to as icons, and so, at an earlier date, were carved ivories, steatites, and sometimes even stone sculptures. None of these was ever really large in size nor ever used in an iconostasis, but the ivories were often gilt and the later metal icons were frequently embellished with pale blue and white enamel. Many of the original moulds produced in the seventeenth century continued to be used until present times, with the result that metal icons of this type are exceedingly difficult to date. Very few of them, however, are able to hold their own in the artistic field beside the panels of even average quality produced by the painters of pre-Petrine Russia.

The wood which was intended for the painted icons had to be carefully chosen, well seasoned and elaborately prepared. At first, only lime, birch, alder and oak were considered suitable, but later cypress was also used. The thickness and size of the panels varied with the purpose for which each icon was intended, as well as with the period and the region in which it was made. Thus, in early times, icons coming from the more heavily wooded districts were generally quite thick, and the painted surfaces were hollowed out. Later, they were comparatively thin, and the margins were painted in imitation of the raised borders of the earlier ones. When necessary, the back of a panel was strengthened against warping by having two hollows cut into it, with an exactly fitting wedge inserted into each. Processional icons which were to be painted on both sides of the board could, for that very reason, not be slatted, and had therefore to be made of thick, well-seasoned and excellent pieces of wood.

The face of the panel had to correspond to the plastered surface of the church walls displaying the mural decorations, of which the icons were in a sense the counterpart. With this end in view the board was covered with a thin layer of gesso, into which powdered alabaster had been worked, and sometimes a layer of canvas incorporated. When the gesso had hardened, it was smoothed down and polished, and only when a glossy surface had been achieved was the panel ready for painting.

The artist worked in tempera, using raw yolk of egg diluted in rye beer as his medium and employing a palette of twenty-four basic colours. His first task consisted in outlining his picture in cinnabar. A coat of white lead paint burnt to a greenish tinge was generally applied to the picture next and the faces painted upon it in a darkish brown, on which the features were then outlined in a reddish ochre, which was in turn touched up with a lighter brown. In this way the shading, or rather the modelling, was produced by the first and darkest coat of paint and not by the topmost one, the process being known as *okhreniye* or 'ochring'. Shadows in the Western sense were unknown, but corresponding effects were produced by various forms of highlights or *bliki;* on the faces these highlights were occasionally carried out in a dark ochre paint mixed with white lead, but more often in white lead paint alone. When they took the form of tiny curved lines, they were known as *ozhyvki* or 'enliveners', but when, as in later times, they consisted of tiny parallel lines, they were called *dvizhki* or 'flecks'. The highlights on draperies were produced by a variety of colours and were known as *probely*.

Specialisation was resorted to in the workshops from a relatively early date, with the result that experienced painters became responsible for the faces only, and in consequence these artists became known as *lichniki* or 'facial artists', whereas their pupils, who came to be called *dolichniki* or 'pre-facial artists', produced the figures and the backgrounds. The scenes were presented either in an architectural setting known as *palaty*, meaning 'chambers' or 'buildings', or against a landscape defined as *gorki*, meaning rocks, because mountainous crags invariably figured in it; interiors were unknown, a canopy or cupola sufficing to indicate that the event had taken place indoors.

The background of an icon was filled in last. It was generally done in gold leaf laid over a priming made of red wine, and was known by the name of *svet* or 'light' because it was meant to represent the radiance of heaven. Sometimes it was damascened, made of a blend of bronze and gold known as *inokop*. For a time, silver backgrounds were also popular in Russia, and, in Novgorod, in the fourteenth century, red backgrounds were used, but soon after, white or rather pale ochre backgrounds became characteristic of the region, whereas green ones were preferred in Pskov and brightish blue ones were sometimes used by the artists of Tver.

The custom of embellishing icons with such precious adornments as metal haloes, jewels, cloisonné enamels and stamped metal sheets was already established in pre-Mongol Kiev; with the passing years it became usual to encase an icon in a costly metal cover or *riza*, in which openings were cut to show the essential sections of the painting. It also became the practice to swathe the icons which were laid upon lecterns with elaborately embroidered cloths which were intended to protect them from dust.

Icon Painters' Guilds in Recent Times

In the first half of the nineteenth century admiration for everything new led to the removal of many old icons from the larger churches of Russia, and but for the zeal with which members of the sect of Old Believers attempted to save the latter from destruction — a zeal which attracted the attention of a small number of art-lovers, inducing them to start collecting icons — Russia would have lost many of the paintings which have today become the chief glory of her medieval art.

The preference shown throughout the nineteenth century for religious paintings of a westernised and more naturalistic character resulted in many icon painters falling out of work. Those who proved unable to adapt themselves to other forms of employment moved to the well-wooded districts of Suzdal and Vladimir, settling for the most part in the villages of Mstera, Palekh and Shuya, where they formed themselves into guilds. Working for the most part from tracings, they turned out large numbers of cheap and generally shoddy icons, but soon the establishment of firms producing even cheaper and more brightly coloured prints reduced the painters to a condition of extreme poverty.

The outbreak of the revolution and the anti-religious measures introduced by the Soviet government put an end to their employment. However, at the dissolution of the guilds the better artists were drafted into workshops established by the new authorities in the same villages, but in which production was switched from icons to that of the lacquer boxes, which today hold a high place among the luxury goods produced in the USSR. Many of the spirited and elegant designs decorating the lids of these delightful caskets are the work of craftsmen who acquired their skill from the icon painters of antiquity, for the calling was usually a hereditary one, a father imparting his secrets to his son. Thus, even though icon painting is no longer practised in the USSR, something of its artistry nevertheless lives on there in a new, if secular, guise.

25

Notes on the Plates

PLATE 1   THE VIRGIN OF VLADIMIR   Constantinopolitan work of the second quarter of the twelfth century. Tretyakov Gallery, Moscow.

This rendering of the Virgin and Child is known in iconography as 'Our Lady of Tenderness'. The icon illustrated on this plate is the earliest panel painting to show it; it is also, assuredly, the loveliest icon as yet known to us. It was specially commissioned from a Constantinopolitan artist, whose name has not survived, by Prince Izyaslav of Kiev, not later than 1132, and reached the Russian capital very soon after that date. Its fate has always been closely linked to Russian history, and it was as a result of political developments that, in 1164, Prince Andrew Bogolyubski transported it to Vladimir, the city from which it takes its name. In 1395, it was moved from the Cathedral of the Assumption at Vladimir to the cathedral of the same name at Moscow, where it remained until 1919, when it was sent to the State Restoration Workshops at Moscow for much needed cleaning and treatment. The work was carried out with great skill, and on its completion the icon was sent to the Tretyakov Gallery in Moscow, where it is now on permanent exhibition.

The original Byzantine panel measures $30\frac{3}{4} \times 21\frac{1}{2}$ inches (78.1 × 54.6 cm.); the margins were added to it later in Russia and have increased its size to $40\frac{3}{4} \times 27$ inches (93.5 × 68.5 cm.). Today only the faces of the original painting survive, but they are of such incomparable beauty that this masterpiece continued to exercise a powerful influence over Russian icon painters throughout the succeeding centuries. The greatest, and they include Andrei Rublev, produced their own renderings of it, and even in this century many have turned to it for inspiration, as well as to admire it as an outstanding work of art.

PLATE 2   THE ARCHANGEL GABRIEL   Russian work of the twelfth century. Russian Museum, Leningrad.

Victor Lazarev ascribes this superb painting, part of a Deesis group, to a royal workshop. It does indeed show Russian painting at its very best, for the profound humanism of this early icon is clearly inspired by the deeply compassionate, yet essentially unsentimental spirit inherent in the Byzantine rendering of the Virgin of Vladimir (see Plate 1). Although the style must have been evolved from that of Constantinople, comparison of the two quickly makes it abundantly clear that the icon under discussion, notwithstanding its early date, is the work of a Russian and not of a Greek artist. The elaborate gold streaking of the hair resulted in this profoundly moving, truly monumental painting often being referred to as the icon of 'The Goldenheaded Angel'.

PLATE 3   ST GEORGE   Novgorodian work of the twelfth century. Cathedral of the Assumption, Moscow.

The iconostasis which was originally provided for the Cathedral of the Assumption in the Kremlin at Moscow was replaced in 1632 by the five-tiered one which is to be seen there today. The icons

26

which fill its four upper tiers date from this later period, but some of those which appear in the bottom tier are far older, and are most probably panels which survive from the earlier iconostasis. Until the revolution, they included the famous Byzantine icon of the Virgin of Vladimir (Plate 1). The superb Novgorodian icon shown here still retains the place which was allotted to it when the new iconostasis was installed in 1632, but its existence was not discovered until after the outbreak of the revolution, when a fourteenth-century painting of the Virgin and Child, which appears on the other face of the panel, was sent to the State Restoration Workshops for treatment. The painting of St George was then first noticed and became the subject of careful restoration.

It is among the very few great works to survive from the pre-Mongol invasion period of Russian art. The saint is shown holding in his right hand a spear ending in a cross, and in his left a sword — at that time the Russian emblem of sovereignty. His robust, forthright yet sympathetic expression and his general air of competence contrast with the otherworldliness of contemporary Greek painting, and are both essentially Russian and typically Novgorodian characteristics. The icon was probably brought to Moscow from the monastery of St George at Novgorod, for which it was undoubtedly painted.

PLATE 4   DEESIS   Late twelfth- or early thirteenth-century work of the Vladimir-Suzdalian school. Formerly in the Cathedral of the Assumption, Moscow, now in the Tretyakov Gallery, Moscow.

The Deesis rendering belongs to the cycle of the Last Judgement, for the figures on either side of the Saviour are interceding with Him on behalf of the damned. It was an extremely popular scene in Vladimir-Suzdalian Russia, where the Virgin came to be regarded, as 'The Hope of the Damned'. Nevertheless, it was precisely at this period that, in the principality of Vladimir-Suzdal, the figures of the Virgin and St John, whom it is usual to see standing on either side of the Saviour with their hands raised in an attitude of supplication, were replaced by two angels. Frequently, too, artists of this school and period were fond of representing the three central figures of the Deesis group on a single panel, as is the case here, rather than on three separate ones.

Very few examples of Vladimir-Suzdalian painting of pre-Mongol invasion date survive, but all that have are of a high quality. The icon illustrated here is a characteristic work — it is imbued with the grace and elegance that are so much a part of the Suzdalian tradition, where they blend poetically with the clarity of conception and artistic integrity which form the basis of every true masterpiece. This painting expresses great intensity of feeling. Christ is shown in early manhood. His delicate features are those of an aristocrat, but the general character of His face stylistically resembles that of the Saviour in the mosaic Deesis scene in the gallery of the Cathedral of Hagia Sophia at Istanbul. But the icon, for all its patrician delicacy, displays a more marked determination to contend with everyday problems than does the Byzantine mosaic. Both the Virgin and St John, though manifesting deep compassion, also show a similar resolution and vitality. Indeed, the painting may well be regarded as a study of human fortitude, expressed with the greatest dignity and restraint.

PLATE 5   ST BORIS AND ST GLEB   Muscovite work of the late fourteenth century. Russian Museum, Leningrad.

The two royal brothers had become almost as popular saints in late fourteenth-century Moscow as they had been for many decades in Novgorodian territory, but at that time the Muscovites looked for guidance in art to the sophisticated, elegant and vital style of Vladimir-Suzdalian Russia, rather than to the more robust school of Novgorod; thus, it is the influence of Suzdalian painting which prevails in the icon illustrated here. In it the royal posture and appearance of the two saints is tempered by their gentle, compassionate expressions: the aquiline nose of a Greek type is, however, retained in their otherwise basically Suzdalian faces, though these are given the rounded eyes and small mouths which are typical of the Muscovite school. Both saints hold the crosses which are the symbols of their calling and the swords which are the badges of their rank. The artist has given full expression to the prevailing taste for decoration by painting the royal costumes worn by the brothers in great detail. Thus, both are shown clothed in identically shaped royal robes, made of differently coloured silks, but adorned with identical embroidered and jewelled trimmings; both wear brocaded robes of different colours, one being trimmed with ermine and the other with squirrel fur, and the costume of both is completed by identically shaped, round caps, edged with sable and made of the same brocade, though cut to produce a different pattern on each headgear.

PLATE 6   THE ARCHANGEL GABRIEL   Pskov work of the first half of the fifteenth century. Russian Museum, Leningrad.

Although this icon was attributed by the late Professor Ellis Minns to Suzdal, cleaning has made it abundantly clear that the painting is a rare and admirable example of early Pskovian workmanship. It comes from the Deesis tier of an iconostasis. In it the Pskovian fondness for sombre, austere colours and severe outlines is clearly to the fore. The solemnity and aloofness of Gabriel's expression receives additional emphasis from the way in which the rocky landscape in the background is made to form a V in order to draw attention to the archangel's sloping shoulders, while at the same time accentuating the importance of his head by allowing it to stand out against the sky. The heart-shaped modelling of the cheekbones is a characteristic feature of the style: when compared with Rublev's treatment (Plate 12), it seems a trifle exaggerated, but it serves to express the inherently graphic approach of Russian artists to painting. Yet this graphic approach has not in this instance led to undue stylisation. The innate feeling for attractive decoration is responsible for the charming trefoil terminal of the archangel's staff and for the style of the medallion. The deep tones of the prevailing green is one of which the people of Pskov were particularly fond; here it is skilfully used to stress the dramatic elements introduced by the triangular shape of the background.

PLATE 7   THE APOSTLES PETER AND PAUL WITH THE CHRIST EMMANUEL   Novgorodian work of the late fourteenth century. $13\frac{1}{4} \times 9\frac{7}{8}$ in. (33.6 × 25 cm.). Hann Collection, USA.

Painted at a time when Novgorod's link with Byzantium was especially strong, this noble work closely follows Byzantine lines, Greek influence expressing itself not only stylistically but also taking the form of a Greek inscription within the medallion displaying the figure of Christ Emmanuel. It is interesting to compare this early representation of two saints with later renderings (see Plates 29 and 30), and to appreciate the classic touch which, in this icon, is responsible for the ample, well-moulded folds of the drapery. The faces of both saints clearly reflect the style which flourished in Constantinople under the Paleologue emperors, and which may well have been introduced to Novgorod first by Theophanes the Greek, who was living and working in that city by 1378, and also by the superb Deesis cycle of icons which was painted in Constantinople only a few years later for the abbot of the Vysotski monastery near Novgorod, and which was delivered to him there before the end of the century.

PLATE 8   ST NICHOLAS THE MIRACLE WORKER WITH SAINTS   Novgorodian work of the late fourteenth or early fifteenth century. $13 \times 10\frac{1}{4}$ in. (33 × 26 cm.). Hann Collection, USA.

The icon is one which follows a tradition, of which the earliest examples so far known are a late twelfth-century icon from the Novodevichi monastery in Moscow and an early thirteenth-century panel from the Dukhov monastery, on which bust-size representations of St Nicholas are surrounded by marginal figures of other saints. On this icon, the centre of the upper margin displays the Deesis, the Saviour's figure in this case taking the form of the Vernicle. Among the seven saints completing the marginal decorations are St Paraskevi and St Alexandra, shown wearing a crown of fifteenth-century shape. The Saviour's representation and that of St Nicholas are painted by a more skilled hand than those responsible for, at any rate, three of the marginal figures. The modelling of St Nicholas's head has been especially carefully carried out.

PLATE 9 THE NATIVITY   Ascribed to Andrei Rublev; 1405. Tretyakov Gallery, Moscow.

This icon has often been called the 'Zvenigorod Nativity', because it came to the Cathedral of the Annunciation at Moscow from that city. It is assuredly the finest Russian rendering of the scene. As prescribed by tradition, the Virgin is shown in the centre, lying extended on a rug at the mouth of the cave, with the Child beside her. The ox and the ass gaze on the Child, and angels guard Him while, above, other angels guide the three kings towards the scene; below, Thyrses informs Joseph of the event while attendants bath the newly born child. The spacing of the scenes, the proportions of the figures, the arrangement and interrelationship of the various groups are all admirably worked out. The luminous and harmonious colours are particularly glowing, and the rocks and vegetation are beautifully rendered, but it is perhaps the almost classic handling of the figures, an element which is to be seen most clearly in the group of maidservants tending the Child, shown at the bottom of the icon, and in that of the mounted kings, who appear at the top of it, which endows this masterpiece with its peculiar beauty and distinction.

PLATE 10   THE VIRGIN OF VLADIMIR   Attributed to Andrei Rublev; *c.* 1408. Russian Museum, Leningrad.

In 1395 Tamerlane advanced into Russia and headed towards Moscow. To face the peril Vasili I, who succeeded his father Dimitri Donskoi in 1389 as Grand Duke of Muscovy, mustered his troops and appealed to the city of Vladimir for the loan of the miraculous Byzantine icon of the Virgin of Vladimir (see Plate 1), for he wished to carry it into battle, both in order to enlist the Virgin's aid and to encourage his men. And, indeed, on the icon's arrival in Moscow Tamerlane unaccountably began to withdraw into Asia, abandoning his assault of Moscow. The capital's escape and the country's deliverance from danger were universally ascribed to the icon's intervention, and the panel was therefore retained in Moscow, where it was installed in the Cathedral of the Assumption in the Kremlin. No documents survive to tell us what the inhabitants of Vladimir felt on being thus dispossessed of their treasure, but early in the fifteenth century the copy of the famous Byzantine icon which is illustrated here was painted to take the place of the original. The new panel proved as fine a work of art in its own way as its prototype; its style is extremely close to Rublev's, and since the master was working in Vladimir in 1408, being primarily engaged on painting the frescoes in the Cathedral of the Assumption there, many eminent authorities attribute this painting to his hand. Its excellence can be more readily appreciated by comparing it with the fine though far less satisfying rendering illustrated on Plate 19.

PLATE 11   THE ANNUNCIATION   Andrei Rublev; 1408. Lime board overlaid with canvas; $55\frac{7}{8} \times 44\frac{3}{4}$ in. (142×114 cm.). Tretyakov Gallery, Moscow.

Originally painted by the artist for the festival tier of the iconostasis of the Cathedral of the Assumption at Vladimir, the icon was transported in 1775 to the church of the village of Vasilievskoe in the county of Ivanov-Vosnessensk, where it remained until the outbreak of the revolution, after which it passed into the state collections.

In icon painting no scenes ever shown take place indoors; the façades of the buildings in which they are supposed to have occurred are used instead to form their backgrounds. The Annunciation is one of the scenes which is always presented in this manner. In this painting the Virgin's head may at first sight appear to be too much inclined, but closer study will soon show how, offset as it is by the complex, rectilinear architectural forms in the background, the curved lines of her head and shoulders serve to focus attention on the commanding figure of the angel, whose rôle in this scene is as important, if not indeed more so than the Virgin's. The rounded roofs of the corner building and the curve of the drapery suspended from one to another of them, maintain the rhythm of the composition in much the same way that the Virgin's inclined body and round halo offset and also harmonise with the architectural character of her throne and the buildings behind it. The superb spacing and the admirable proportions of the figures, their gentle nobility, their emotional power and also their serenity clearly reflect a master's hand. The lovely colours are blended and balanced with equal skill, and a profound and moving spirituality pervades the scene. This icon is as fine as a better known version of the Annunciation, painted by Rublev in 1405 for the Cathedral of the Annunciation at Moscow, and there is no reason for questioning the attribution of the present panel to the same artist.

PLATE 12   THE CENTRAL ANGEL FROM THE OLD TESTAMENT TRINITY   by Andrei Rublev; 1411. Lime board overlaid with canvas; $55\frac{7}{8} \times 46\frac{1}{2}$ in. $(142 \times 118$ cm.). Tretyakov Gallery, Moscow.

The second half of the fourteenth century owed much of its cultural and spiritual development to the influence of three outstanding clerics: one of them, St Sergius of Radonezh, founded in 1337, on a site to the northeast of Moscow, in the village which is known today as Zagorsk, the Monastery of the Trinity and St Sergius. Under his direction, it soon became the largest monastery in Great Russia and an important centre of icon painting, for Sergius, who was anxious to foster a rebirth of the arts, provided it with its own workshops. Andrei Rublev became a monk at this monastery while Sergius was still its superior, and probably received most of his artistic training in its workshops. He painted the icon of the Old Testament Trinity in 1411, when he returned to the monastery after working in Vladimir and in Moscow, to commemorate Sergius, who had died but recently. The icon was intended to occupy a place above the saint's tomb, within a cathedral which was being built over the grave.

The painting is Rublev's masterpiece. It has often been reproduced in its entirety in Western publications: this detail contains the essence of Rublev's magic, conveying a clear impression of his profoundly spiritual yet restrained and entirely unsentimental approach. Its deeply emotional power depends largely on the skill with which Rublev selected his soft yet deep and essentially luminous colours, blending them to produce extremely harmonious effects while, at the same time, setting off the grace of his firm yet delicate and flowing line. His artistic sensibility is easier to appreciate if the heartshaped modelling of his angel's face is compared with that of the archangel Gabriel illustrated on Plate 6, for Rublev has refrained from unduly emphasising the convention, and has skilfully used the shading round the eyes and along the sides of the face to express the angel's introspective mood.

PLATE 13   ST JOHN   Largely the work of Andrei Rublev; 1408. Tretyakov Gallery Moscow.

The icon originally belonged to the Deesis tier of the iconostasis in the Cathedral of the Assumption at Vladimir. It is exceptionally large, measuring approximately 10 ft. $3\frac{5}{8}$ in. (3 metres 14 cm.) in height. Thus, it exceeds by about one metre the large icons which Theophanes the Greek was in the habit of painting, thereby reflecting one aspect of the influence which he exerted over Rublev. Rublev designed all the icons required for the Deesis tier of this iconostasis, but although all were produced under his direction, the only one which is wholly by his hand is that of the Saviour. He contributed to the other panels in differing degrees. The painting shown here bears many characteristics that are essentially his, and it is so deeply impregnated with his spirit that even if it is not entirely his work it must be recognised as, at any rate, very largely so.

PLATE 14   AN ANGEL FROM AN OLD TESTAMENT TRINITY   School of Rublev; late fourteenth century. Cathedral of the Assumption, Moscow.

This detail shows the head of one of the angels in an icon of an Old Testament Trinity, which was retained in the later iconostasis belonging to the Cathedral of the Assumption at Moscow from the earlier one. Until 1945, when it was sent to the workshops for cleaning, it displayed an eighteenth-century overpainting; the original work is of the very highest order. Its superb colours are blended with a delicacy which recalls that of Rublev's hand, but the forthright expression of the angel, with its absence of marked ethereality, harks back to the traditions of pre-Mongol invasion days, forming a link with paintings such as that of the St Gorge illustrated on Plate 3.

PLATE 15 A BIOGRAPHICAL ICON OF ST GEORGE Novgorodian work of the fourteenth century. Russian Museum, Leningrad.

Biographical icons became extremely popular in fourteenth and fifteenth-century Russia. In some, the strictly iconic style was adhered to; in others, the folklorist element was allowed expression, when it was often combined with details of costume or furniture drawn from contemporary life. The Novgorodian icon illustrated here is a spirited example of the iconic style, enlivened by touches of genre elements. Each of the small scenes is imbued with the artist's mastery of the problems of spacing and proportion, and by his ability to invest his somewhat unsophisticated interpretations with clarity and dignity. The central representation, as is usual in icons of this type, is considerably larger in size than the scenes which frame it; it displays a greater elegance and subtlety than do the rather more archaic subsidiary scenes. It presents a lithe and graceful St George, astride a prancing, extremely fine horse, being welcomed by the princess who holds the lead of a vanquished, rather heraldic looking dragon, while her parents watch the scene from the town's battlements. St George's face, like that of the princess and her parents, is treated in a markedly naturalistic manner, and this naturalistic approach is reflected anew in the period costumes worn by the princess and her parents, as well as in the characteristically Novgorodian appearance of the architecture.

The scenes forming the border are archaic in conception, but their genre elements are in keeping with the taste of their own time. Starting from left to right, in the top margin we see 1. St George distributing his possessions to the poor; 2. soldiers lead him bound; 3. they conduct him to the emperor; 4. they imprison him; on the left border 5. they torture him on a wheel; 6. they flay him with hooks; 7. they rub him with stones; on the opposite border 8. St George casts down idols; 9. he is beaten; 10. he is burnt with torches; along the lower margin 11. St George is boiled; 12. he is wounded with a saw; 13. stones are piled round him, and he is drenched with water; 14. he is dismembered with a sword.

PLATE 16 ST PARASKEVI Novgorodian work of the early fifteenth century. $12\frac{1}{4} \times 10\frac{5}{8}$ in. (31.1 × 27.2 cm.). Hann Collection, USA.

This fine example of fifteenth-century Novgorodian painting shows St Paraskevi, the patron saint of the sick and ailing, holding a metal vessel, probably containing a life-giving tonic, in her left hand and a cross in her right. The painting follows the best Novgorodian traditions, the silhouette-like outlines of the figure combined with the gentle yet forthright manner of its presentation and the absence of all unnecessary details conforming to the austere standards of taste which characterise much of the work of the period. The icon's colour scheme is restrained, almost reduced to monochrome, but a powerful effect is produced by the use of cinnabar on the saint's robe and of white for her head covering. The jewelled bands which decorate her garments contribute a touch of elegance, which is sustained by the delicate features of her face and her serious yet serene expression. It is not usual for a saint's halo to protrude as it does here from the face of the icon onto its frame-like border.

PLATE 17 CHRIST ENTHRONED Muscovite work of the early fifteenth century. 42 × 31 in. (106.6 × 78.7 cm.). Hann Collection, USA.

This traditional presentation of the Saviour enthroned must originally have formed the central panel of a Deesis group. Christ is shown seated on a throne of a typically fifteenth-century type, holding in His left hand a Bible open at the text, 'Come unto me and be justly judged'. A mandorla surrounds Him, filled with cherubim, while the emblems of the apostles occupy triangular sections protruding at the corners. The figure is noble, indeed majestic, the drapery dynamic and splendidly modelled. Novgorodian influence is responsible for the fine colour scheme and that of Theophanes the Greek for the faces of the cherubim, but the Saviour is given the small, rounded ead and delicate features characteristic of early fifteenth-century Muscovite work. This is a fine example of the sort of icon which, following in the Rublev-Danila Cherny tradition, was probably typical of the early Muscovite school, but which is now a rarity, the majority of the panels belonging to this period having perished in the great fire of 1547.

PLATE 18   THE VIRGIN OF TENDERNESS   Pskov; early fifteenth century. 13⅜ × 11 in. (34 × 28 cm.). Hann Collection, USA.

This rendering of the Virgin and Child is derived from that introduced into iconography by the icon of the Virgin of Vladimir, but in it the element of affection linking Mother and Child is far more strongly stressed than in the original version. Here the use of triple white lines to indicate the highlights recall those on the icon of four saints shown on Plate 23; but whereas the brilliant colours which appear in the latter are typical of the Novgorodian school, the sombre tones of this panel and the modelling of the faces are characteristic of Pskovian painting. The figures of the Virgin and Child are surrounded by those of thirteen saints. Starting from the top left-hand corner, those on the top register represent St Nicholas, St George, St Demetrius and St Paraskevi; St Peter and Elijah appear on the left panel; St Paul and St John on the right; St Blaise, St Anastasia, St Florus, St Laurus and St Cosmas along the bottom.

PLATE 19   THE VIRGIN OF VLADIMIR   Novgorodian work of the second half of the fifteenth century. 34¼ × 24½ in. (87 × 62 cm.). Hann Collection, USA.

This extremely lovely Novgorodian version of the icon of the Virgin of Vladimir closely follows the lines of its Byzantine prototype, though it expresses the Child's affection for His mother more clearly than does the original. The Virgin's figure retains the silhouette-like outline peculiar to rather earlier Novgorodian paintings, though the schematic treatment of the drapery and, more especially, the treatment of the Child's robe are typical of the later fifteenth century. Though no trace of the influence of Theophanes is to be found in the treatment of the central theme, its effect can be observed in the lovely little rendering of the Old Testament Trinity, carried out in tones of blue-greys, in the centre of the icon's upper margin; it must be attributed to a different hand from that responsible for the figures of the Virgin and Child, which reflect the influence of Rublev rather than of Theophanes.

The tiny scenes which occupy the upper corners of the icon are by yet another hand; both may be a decade or so later in date than the main painting. The rendering of St John is closer to Byzantine tradition than that showing the Descent into Hell; the latter displays superb grouping. The fine metal frame dates from the turn of the sixteenth century.

PLATE 20   THE HOLY WISDOM   Novgorodian work of mid- to late-fifteenth-century date. 16⅝ × 13⅜ in. (42.2 × 34 cm.). Hann Collection, USA.

Not only were churches dedicated to Hagia Sophia, the Holy Wisdom of God, and thus to the Saviour, but paintings illustrating this theme were also quite often produced, the earliest known in Russia being a fresco dated 1363, in the church at Volotovo, near Novgorod. In painting, the Holy Wisdom is represented in the form of a winged female figure who is generally shown seated on a throne set against a gloriole or mandorla, wearing a crown. In this icon, the Saviour in a gloriole looks down from above, while angels grouped round a centrally placed altar fill the top of the icon. The Virgin, holding a medallion, and St John stand on either side of the Holy Wisdom, who wears a jewelled robe and a crown of late-fifteenth-century date. The rather dark tones of the icon and the band of angels in the sky seem to foreshadow some of the trends which characterise Muscovite painting of the latter part of the sixteenth century.

PLATE 21   QUADRIPARTITE ICON ILLUSTRATING SCENES FROM THE PASSION   Novgorodian work of the mid-fifteenth century. 22 × 16½ in. (55.8 × 41.9 cm.). Hann Collection, USA.

32

This very fine icon shows, from left to right, the Flagellation, the Mockery of Christ, Christ carrying the Cross and the Crucifixion. In many ways, it resembles an early fifteenth-century quadripartite icon in the Russian Museum at Leningrad, showing the Raising of Lazarus, the Old Testament Trinity, the Purification of the Virgin and John the Evangelist dictating his Gospel to Prokhorus, but in the present painting the soldiers wear helmets and uniforms similar to those shown in the icon illustrating the battle fought between the men of Novgorod and those of Suzdal, which was painted in about 1480. It is for this reason, as well as because of the rectilinear lines of the buildings appearing in the backgrounds of the scenes, that a date towards the middle of the fifteenth century seems the more likely one for this icon. There is much in this painting to arouse admiration: the grouping and spacing of the figures is superb; the outlines are clear yet flowing and harmonious; the sense of colour greatly developed; and the feeling for decoration and dramatic effect well marked. Especially to be noted is the composition of the lower scenes, the lines of the crosses in the one being skilfully disposed to create an impression of movement, the massive horizontal lines of the great cross in the other being contrasted with the angular lines formed by Christ's arms, so as to accentuate the dramatic content of the scene.

PLATE 22   AN INCIDENT FROM THE MARTYRDOM OF ST GEORGE   Provincial work in the Novgorodian style; fifteenth century. $10\frac{1}{2} \times 6\frac{3}{4}$ in. (26.6 × 17.1 cm.). Hann Collection, USA.

This small scene probably appeared originally as one of a series forming the margins of a biographical icon of St George. It shows the saint being wounded by saws. His torturers wear headdresses which are typical of the period, and the architectural background is equally characteristic of the age and school. But the artist has set out to produce an arresting composition by contrasting the perpendicular lines of the buildings and the upright figures of the torturers with the horizontal lines of the body of the martyred saint.

PLATE 23   FOUR SAINTS   Novgorodian school; early fifteenth century. $19\frac{1}{8} \times 13\frac{3}{4}$ in. (48.5 × 34.9 cm.). Hann Collection, USA.

Seen from left to right, the saints represented on this panel are the apostles Peter and Paul, and St Cosmas and St Damian. The figures still retain the frontal pose and direct presentation, combined with the exclusion of all subsidiary details, which characterise early Novgorodian works. The schematic treatment of the drapery with, above all, the use of highlights in the form of three parallel lines marking the forehead and cheekbones of the faces, as well as the white outlines to the ears, are stylistic peculiarities which appear in the latter part of the fourteenth century and persist during the opening decades of the fifteenth, though, by the end of the latter century, the white lines usually become fused into a brush stroke forming a white highlight.

PLATE 24   A BIOGRAPHICAL ICON OF ST NICHOLAS   Novgorodian work of the fifteenth century. Russian Museum, Leningrad.

The portrait of St Nicholas follows the traditional lines laid down in the twelfth century, as is the case of the icon illustrated on Plate 8, but medallions bearing busts of the Saviour and the Virgin have been included. The workmanship is accomplished, and the colours are good. The scenes show, starting with the top border, the saint's birth, his baptism, an event which is difficult to identify but may well show him being received into the church, being taken to learn to read, his ordination as a deacon; the left margin illustrates his ordination as archbishop, his appearance to Constantine in a dream, saving three men from the sword; the paintings on the right border display him saving a ship from foundering, appearing to three imprisoned men, buying a piece of stuff from a Tyrian merchant; below, he gives the piece of stuff to a poor woman, he saves Demetrius from drowning, he saves Basil's son Agricul from the Saracens, he is placed in his coffin and his bones are removed to Bari for reinterment there in 1087.

PLATE 25   THE CENTRAL SECTION OF A BIOGRAPHICAL ICON OF THE ARCHANGEL MICHAEL $92\frac{1}{2} \times$ $71\frac{1}{2}$ in. (235 × 182 cm.). First half of the fifteenth century. Cathedral of the archangel Michael, Moscow.

In Russia, St Michael was regarded as the protector of princes and warriors, and he is shown here wearing full military panoply; he holds a sword in one hand, and with his extended wings he appears as the very embodiment of knightly grace and valour, as well as of the saintly virtues. Notwithstanding their small size, the scenes which frame his figure and which illustrate events from his life are dramatic and monumental in style. It is unfortunate that time has dealt harshly with many of them; however, others, such as that on the right border, showing Jacob's fight with the Angel, or that in the lower border, of King David's repentance, are still in good condition. The influence of Rublev is clearly to the fore in this icon, but many of the scenes are rendered in a more dynamic manner than the master's, and the painting is the work of an artist who was also deeply affected by the forcefulness of Theophanes's style.

PLATE 26   ST GEORGE AND THE DRAGON   Novgorodian work of the late fifteenth century. $16 \times 13\frac{1}{8}$ in. (40.6 × 33.3 cm.). Formerly in the Tretyakov Gallery, Moscow, now in the Hann Collection, USA.

This particularly decorative painting combines several unusual features, for although the saint and his horse follow lines that are characteristic of fifteenth-century Novgorodian painting, the treatment of the hills suggests a provincial, northern school, while the elaboration with which the town's gateway is shown foreshadows later Muscovite developments. The princess leads the dragon by a cord as it emerges from its cave, while her parents and their attendants watch the scene from the tower, and townsmen look on from the battlements. The Saviour blesses the saint from a festoon of clouds, while His angelic emissary places a crown upon the saint's head. The angel's pose, paralleled as it is by the horizontal line of the saint's spear, gives the composition an unusual feeling of movement and rhythm; indeed, the decorative quality of this icon and its spirited composition are of the very highest order.

PLATE 27   ST DEMETRIUS   Vladimir-Suzdalian work of the late fifteenth century. Hann Collection, USA.

This decorative icon of St Demetrius, seated on a brocaded cushion laid on a stool-shaped throne, shows the saint wearing a warrior's costume. He holds a cross in his right hand, and a round, richly decorated metal shield in his left. The spacing and arrangement of the scene is admirable, and the saint's figure is full of nobility. Both the style of his face and that of the churches appearing in the background confirm the late A. Aviroff's attribution of the painting to the Vladimir-Suzdalian school. The relatively late date he assigned to it is borne out, on the one hand, by the architectural features and by the artist's interest in decoration, as well as by the treatment of the foreground, which includes a debased rendering of the convention used in early Novgorodian painting to depict mountains, but which has lost its meaning here and come to be used to create a flat but patterned piece of ground. The repoussé metal frame is a later addition, dating from the first half of the seventeenth century.

PLATE 28   A BIOGRAPHICAL ICON OF ST BASIL   Late-fifteenth-century work, perhaps by a provincial artist working in Moscow. $32\frac{1}{4} \times 27\frac{3}{4}$ in. (81.9 × 70.4 cm.). Hann Collection, USA.

As the late A. Aviroff pointed out in his catalogue of the Hann Collection, the churches represented in the backgrounds of the marginal scenes are so like the domed ones of the Vladimir-Suzdalian area that the artist responsible for the paintings must have been well acquainted with the architectural style of that region. However, some of the buildings belonging to the scenes in the lower margin are typical of the style evolved in Novgorod and the northern provinces. Furthermore, whereas the rocks are stylised in a manner which is altogether different from that followed by Novgorodian and Muscovite artists, other features, more especially the interest taken in vestments and in

34

curved lines, are typical of the Novgorodian school, while preoccupation with architectural forms reflects Muscovite taste. It is therefore tempting to ascribe the icon to a Novgorodian artist working in the capital at a time when the Muscovites were being influenced by the art of the Vladimir-Suzdalian area.

PLATE 29   ST BASIL AND ST NICHOLAS   Novgorodian work of the turn of the fifteenth century. Each icon approximately 32¾ × 14¾ in. (83.1 × 37.5 cm.). Hann Collection, USA.

These icons probably came from the Deesis tier of the same iconostasis, and must originally have had an ochre background which was later overpainted in pale blue. Dating from the time when the interest in church vestments was at its height, both saints are shown wearing bishop's robes adorned with a cruciform pattern. While the figures retain the inclined pose proper to saints figuring in the Deesis cycle, there is something a trifle mannered in their appearance which points to a relatively late date for the paintings. Nevertheless, the general effect is one of grandeur, and the mood of the painting remains humanistic and essentially compassionate, whereas later icons of this type often strike a more impersonal note, and set out to produce a rather more sumptuous effect.

PLATE 30   ST MACARIUS OF ALEXANDRIA AND ST MACARIUS OF EGYPT   School of Rublev; late sixteenth century. 12½ × 9½ in. (31.7 × 24.1 cm.). Hann Collection, USA.

St Macarius of Alexandria wears bishop's robes, while the saint who elected to live as a hermit in the Egyptian desert, like many an early anchorite, has only his long beard with which to cover his nakedness. Both figures have the sloping shoulders and silhouette-like outlines which are special characteristics of Rublev's style. The background of the painting is filled with wavy lines representing clouds forming an integral part of the picture's composition. A medallion, containing a representation of Christ in the act of blessing, is set in the centre of the top of the icon, and it is balanced below by a small, delicately drawn bush which completes the composition and reflects the influence of Rublev. It is very difficult to determine the date of this painting; the icon is an almost identical version of that published by Solntzev in 1849, in the first volume of 'The Antiquities of the Russian Empire' (in Russian), and which is described by Likhachev, in the pre-revolutionary catalogue of the Hermitage Museum, as a seventeenth-century Novgorodian work. If so, the painting is a surprisingly archaic one. The exactitude with which the bishop's vestments are shown and the way in which his face is painted make a date somewhere around 1590 seem the most likely, with a Muscovite follower of Rublev's, rather than one of the Novgorodian tradition, a more probable attribution.

PLATE 31   THE TRANSFIGURATION   Novgorodian work of the second half of the fifteenth century. 32½ × 23¾ in. (82.5 × 60.3 cm.). Formerly in the Tretyakov Gallery, Moscow, now in the Hann Collection, USA.

This lovely painting closely follows the traditional lines prescribed by Byzantine iconography. Above, it shows Christ set against a six-pointed star, surrounded by a gloriole, with Elijah and Moses standing on rocky peaks on either side of Him. Three rays emanating from behind Christ's body direct attention to the startled apostles seen below. The delicate yet firm character of the drawing is balanced in this painting by the truly superb colours, the admirable proportions of the figures to the whole, and the spacing of the two groups of people. The poses of the apostles and their startled expressions contrast with the quiet majesty of the figures shown above and produce a dramatic effect, but much of the distinction of the painting is due to the skilful way in which their bodies are foreshortened.

PLATE 32   ST JOSEPH   Northern work of the turn of the fourteenth century. Hann Collection, USA.

This is a detail from a larger icon which probably represented the Nativity. It is of particular interest because it illustrates the survival of classical elements in Russian religious art of late medieval date. But for the halo and the markedly Russian character of Joseph's face, we might well be looking at the figure of some ancient philosopher as depicted in Hellenistic art. Though the figure is skilfully drawn and the draperies ably rendered, the fact that neither of Joseph's hands is visible, coupled with the presence of a Greek instead of a Russian inscription on what is undoubtedly a Russian work, suggests that the figure may well have been copied from a Byzantine illumination. On the other hand, the rocks are rendered in the customary Novgorodian manner, and the face is outlined in white and modelled with white highlights, a style popular in Novgorod at this time.

Yet, for all his ability, the painter lacked keen perceptive powers, and, as a result, the naturalistic, almost portrait-like treatment of the face fails to accord fully with the convention followed both in the composition of the picture and in the treatment of the drapery. When this is considered in conjunction with the square shape of the protruding foot, which closely resembles the treatment of the feet seen in the icon illustrated on Plate 35, an attribution to a provincial, probably a northern artist working in the Novgorodian tradition, seems probable. Joseph's animals are painted in a style which often appears in Novgorodian manuscript illuminations of a similar date.

PLATE 33   ST NICHOLAS THE WONDER WORKER   Muscovite work of the fifteenth century. 18 × 14½ in. (45.7 × 36.8 cm.). Hann Collection, USA.

Iconographically, this fine icon closely adheres to an early prototype, yet, stylistically, it is wholly of its period, for the saint's silhouette-like figure and sloping shoulders are largely the result of Rublev's influence, whereas the elongated proportions of his body are inspired by Dionysius. The careful painting of his face, where the symmetrical treatment is enlivened by modelling designed to create a rhythmical effect, is as typical of Muscovite painting of the latter half of the fifteenth century as is the icon's severe, somewhat sombre colouring; indeed, the modelling helps to offset the decorative treatment of his beard and hair. The roundels on either side of the saint's head were probably intended to contain busts of the Saviour and the Virgin or of the purchaser's patron saints. Though in this respect the icon is incomplete, the figure of St Nicholas is a finished, careful and highly accomplished painting.

PLATE 34   THE DEESIS CYCLE   Novgorodian school; turn of the fifteenth century. Formerly in the Tretyakov Gallery, Moscow, now in the Hann Collection, USA.

Though the figure of the Saviour flanked by those of the Virgin and St John symbolise the Deesis, the customary cycle includes at least four additional figures, and often many more. The four additional, basic figures consist of the archangels Gabriel and Michael, and the apostles Peter and Paul, the group of seven forming what is known as a *chin* or 'order'. The *chin* shown here is an important work which closely adheres to traditional lines. The silhouette-like outlines and inclined heads of the outer figures reflect the persistence of Rublev's influence in works where, as here, the faces follow Byzantine tradition. The colours in all seven panels are good, but the schematic treatment of the drapery and the look of alertness in the figure of Christ, as well as the decorative considerations responsible for the manner in which He is presented, all reflect Muscovite taste. The panels may well have been painted by a Novgorodian artist who had come under Muscovite influence when the presence of Italian artists in the capital was arousing widespread interest.

PLATE 35   THE ASCENSION   Northern school; late fifteenth century. 22½ × 15 in. (57.1 × 38.1 cm.). Hann Collection, USA.

This rendering differs from the more usual form illustrated on Plate 38, though it shows the Virgin standing in her customary place between two white-robed angels, with the apostles and some saints gathered round them, while Christ in a gloriole looks down upon them from heaven. In this instance, however, the gloriole enclosing Christ is not supported by two angels shown in the position given to winged victories in classical art, as seen on Plate 38; instead, they uphold it from behind, so that only their heads and shoulders appear on either side of it. Furthermore, instead of being set in a flat landscape, groups of mountains rise up on either side of the painting leaving a V-shaped section of sky to serve as a background for the central figures, so as to focus attention upon them.

The style of this painting is very close to that to be seen in two fine icons* which are now in the Tretyakov Gallery, Moscow, and which were formerly in the Ostroukhov Collection. The present painting is to be ascribed to an earlier, that is to say, to a late-fifteenth-century date, rather than to the sixteenth century to which the two Tretyakov panels are dated, with the influence of Pskov predominating, rather than that of Novgorod, as in the case of the latter.

PLATE 36   THE DORMITION   Novgorodian work of the turn of the fifteenth century. Formerly in the Morozov Collection in the Tretyakov Gallery, Moscow, now in the Hann Collection, USA.

This is the customary rendering of the scene, showing the Virgin on her bier, surrounded by saintly mourners, while the Saviour in a mandorla, or glory, appears behind her holding her soul in the form of a tiny child. The treatment of the subject is essentially linear, the Virgin's body forming a strongly marked curve, the movement of which is reflected in the bowed figures of many of the mourners. The sombre colouring and the profusion of gold hatchings, as well as the artist's preoccupation with vestments and the elongation to which the figures have been subjected, denote a relatively late work, though one which closely adheres to earlier traditions.

PLATE 37   THE ANNUNCIATION   Novgorodian work of the latter half of the fifteenth century. $10\frac{3}{4} \times 8\frac{1}{2}$ in. (27.3 × 21.5 cm.). Formerly in the Morozov Collections in the Tretyakov Gallery, Moscow, now in the Hann Collection, USA.

This is a fine example of the traditional rendering of the Annunciation, with the angel approaching the seated Virgin from the left, showing the latter facing him with her hands raised in the customary gesture of astonishment. The buildings seen in the background are characteristic of fifteenth-century Novgorodian painting, but the profuse use of white highlights on the drapery of the angel's garments suggests a date in the latter part, rather than the earlier half of the century.

PLATE 38   THE ASCENSION   mid-sixteenth century.* $11\frac{1}{4} \times 9\frac{3}{4}$ in. (28.5 × 24.7 cm.). Hann Collection, USA.

This version of the Ascension is closer to Byzantine tradition than that shown on Plate 35, because the angels supporting the gloriole are extended in the posture of flying victories; yet whereas it is more usual for earth and sky to meet in a straight line on the horizon, here a row of hills intervenes. However, the straight line of the horizon is maintained, and the trees which belong to the traditional flat skyline rise above the hills to conform to precedent. The green of the sky is a colour which is typical of Pskov, but the rocks are painted according to the Novgorodian manner known as *piatochki*, meaning 'tiny foot soles'. The influence of Dionysius is responsible for the elongated proportions of the figures and their manner of standing poised on tiptoe, but their rather stiff postures point to a provincial hand. The figure of Christ in the gloriole is, on the other hand, painted in the Muscovite manner, and the gold hatchings in the gloriole also conform to trends current in the capital towards the middle and latter parts of the sixteenth century.

The attractive metal frame is of early seventeenth-century date.

PLATE 39   SMALL ICONOSTASIS   Novgorodian school; turn of the fifteenth century. $6\frac{3}{4} \times 19$ in. (17.1 × 48.2 cm.). Hann Collection, USA.

The icon is divided into two horizontal bands, the lower of which, as the more important, occupies some two-thirds of the panel's width. The scene in this lower section reproduces a fairly large Deesis cycle. It shows the Saviour at the centre, seated on a throne of fifteenth-century date; the Virgin and St John stand in their customary positions on either side of Him, flanked by the archangels

* Plates 39 and 40, *Icons*, T. Talbot Rice, Batchworth Press, London

Gabriel and Michael, and four saints. The late A. Aviroff identified two of the latter as St Zosima and St Sabbatius, the founders of the Solovetsk monastery on the White Sea. In the upper section of the icon, a rendering of the Virgin of the Sign occupies the central position, with four prophets ranged on either side of her. The colours and spacing of this painting remain good, but once again the rather stiff figures of the saints suggest a provincial artist of considerable skill, rather than one from Novgorod itself.

PLATE 40   THE OLD TESTAMENT TRINITY.   Moscow; sixteenth century. Tretyakov Gallery, Moscow.

This iconographic version of the Old Testament Trinity had long been popular in Russia when the Council of the Hundred Chapters, which met in Moscow in 1551, instructed painters to turn to Rublev's icon on this theme for guidance and inspiration. This icon closely conforms to the prescribed lines, for it shows the three angels symbolising the Trinity seated at the table set with food and drink. In this instance, radishes are laid on it for them, and vessels of contemporary shape contain other forms of refreshment. The figures of the angels have been considerably elongated to conform to the proportions introduced by Dionysius, but the folds of their draperies, the pensive expressions on their faces, and their inclined heads and sloping shoulders are in the Rublev tradition. Their silver haloes are adorned with inset jewels, and the icon's embossed frame dates from the turn of the sixteenth century.

PLATE 41   THE ANNUNCIATION.   Muscovite painting of the transitional period. $16 \times 12\frac{3}{4}$ in. (40.6×32.3 cm.). Hann Collection, USA.

This spirited rendering of the Annunciation combines so many Novgorodian and Muscovite elements that the panel may well have been painted in the latter part of the sixteenth century, when many Novgorodian artists were employed in Moscow, often sharing workshops belonging to their Muscovite colleagues. The scene is set against a complex, largely naturalistic, architectural background of Muscovite style, but the red drapery derived from classical times and retained by the Novgorodians to indicate that the scene was occurring indoors, still appears; its position is, however, less prominent. The figure of the angel also closely follows an ancient Novgorodian tradition of Byzantine origin; but whereas the Virgin's body has the sloping shoulders and elongated proportions which characterise the works of Rublev's followers, her face is rendered in the Muscovite manner, and her rather awkward pose as she turns away in distress is also characteristic of later Muscovite work. The sombre colouring, the schematic treatment of the drapery and the geometric shapes assumed by many of the white highlights are also typical of this period and school. The fine metal frame is several decades later in date than the painting, and is probably to be assigned to the turn of the century.

PLATE 42   THE THREE MARYS AT THE SEPULCHRE.   Moscow; latter part of the sixteenth century. $12\frac{1}{2} \times 10\frac{3}{4}$ in. (31.7×27.3 cm.). Hann Collection, USA.

The scene is set against a background, the elaborate nature of which is characteristic both of the school and the period. The white flecking used to indicate the rocks produces a less regular and a rather more natural effect than that attained by the method adopted by Novgorodian painters. While the three Marys and their companions approach the empty tomb over which an angel stands guard, the resurrected Christ appears in the upper part of the icon. The group of soldiers seen on the left wear the type of dress in which soldiers are portrayed in contemporary manuscript illuminations, but the composition of the icon is unusually complex, the curved lines of the inclined figures being accentuated and re-echoed in the shape of the haloes, in order to counterbalance the outlines formed by the hills. Furthermore, the numerous figures are so cleverly disposed in the small amount of space available that all feeling of overcrowding is avoided, and the larger size assigned by convention to the Saviour's representation is so skilfully worked out that it does not disturb the harmony of the composition nor disrupt the proportions of the whole.

PLATE 43 THE RAISING OF LAZARUS Moscow; turn of the sixteenth century. 12⅜ × 10¾ in. (31.4 × 27.3 cm.). Hann Collection, USA.

This is a good example of average Muscovite painting of a relatively late date, displaying the love of symmetry, balance and decoration typical of the school. The horizontal lines formed by the figures of Christ and the apostles grouped behind Him are balanced by those of the risen Lazarus and an attendant, while the pattern created by the outlines of the three women kneeling at Christ's feet is offset by that of the town gates above, with a group of citizens gathered outside them. The hills are formed by means of the irregular highlights typical of the Muscovite school, while the elongation of the figures, and their way of standing on tiptoe, points to the influence of Dionysius, though the modelling of their faces, with the stress laid on their cheekbones, recalls the manner of Rublev's companion, Danila Cherny, and the latter's followers. The inscription is in Greek and Slavonic, and the metal frame is almost contemporary in date.

PLATE 44 THE VIRGIN AND CHILD Moscow; turn of the sixteenth century. 12¾ × 11 in. (32.3 × 28 cm.). Hann Collection, USA.

Iconographically, this rendering of the Mother and Child is known by the name of the 'Virgin Hodegetria', or 'Pointer of the Way', because she indicates the Child with the right hand, while Christ performs the blessing with His. Though this closely follows the form laid down by Byzantine tradition, the features of the Virgin's face clearly reflect the effect of the Western influences which were reaching Moscow from Europe at this time. However, the Child's face continues to conform to the iconographic style, but the profuse use of gold hatchings, used to indicate the folds of His robe, are characteristic of later Muscovite painting. The beautiful silver filigree and enamel haloes are adorned with precious stones, and display the fine workmanship achieved at that time; the embossed metal frame is of a very slightly later date.

PLATE 45 ST LEONTIUS Possibly school of Tver; late sixteenth century. 11⅛ × 9½ in. (28 × 24.1 cm.). Formerly in the Tretyakov Gallery, now in the Hann Collection, USA.

The markedly dramatic feeling of this painting, combined with its obvious concern with decoration, as well as its monumental character, all suggest a school of high quality, though one which was affected by trends which were fashionable at the time in Moscow. Yaroslavl or Tver would seem likely places of origin, and although very little is known as yet about the school of Tver, the absence of any subsidiary details of a decorative character, such as were customary at Yaroslavl, and the attention devoted to the portrayal of the vestments, which in this case appear to be made of contemporary stuffs, would make Tver the more likely attribution. This would also help to account for the slightly archaic treatment of the saint's face.

The embossed metal frame and covering are of a slightly later date than the icon, belonging to the opening decades of the seventeenth century.

PLATE 46 TRIPTYCH SHOWING THE VIRGIN AND CHILD WITH SCRIPTURAL SCENES Moscow; turn of the sixteenth century. Central panel, 25½ × 21½ in. (64.7 × 54.6 cm.). Hann Collection, USA.

The central panel of this icon is characteristic of the work which was being done at the turn of the sixteenth century by artists employed by the sovereign and his court in the workshops at the Palace of Arms, Moscow. Iconographically, this rendering is known as that of the 'Virgin of Kazan', being a variant of the Virgin Hodegetria. The central figures are surrounded by an embossed metal frame, and they are decked with metal haloes, surmounted in the Virgin's case by a crown and including a collar, or *zata*, set with stones; these are contemporary with the painting. The scenes which surround the central figures are painted in what is often described as the Stroganov style and is probably the work of a different artist, for it was not unusual at the time for two artists to combine their skill on a single panel.

The small scene above the central figures presents the Trinity, with the Virgin and St John appearing beside the symbols of the evangelists. The left wing of the triptych shows the birth of the Virgin above, with below, seen from left to right, her presentation in the Temple and the Annunciation, the Baptism and the Raising of Lazarus, the Crucifixion and the Descent into Hell, the Old Testament Trinity and the Virgin's Dormition. The right panel shows the Glorification of the Virgin above, with, below, the Nativity and the Presentation in the Temple, the Entry into Jerusalem and the Transfiguration, the Three Marys at the Empty Tomb and the Ascension, the Raising of the True Cross and Our Lady of Protection.

PLATE 47 THE VISION OF EULOGIUS · Moscow; sixteenth century. Russian Museum, Leningrad.

In the sixteenth century, Russian icon painters started to illustrate mystical and didactic themes such as that shown on the present panel. The theme chosen here expresses a monastery's concern for the needs of the poor. The painting shows the interior of a walled monastery. The tower, probably its entrance gate, in the background is reproduced with considerable architectural fidelity, and suffices to suggest the appearance of the remaining walls. Within the enclosure, a fine domed church of Muscovite style and its forecourt occupy much of the background. The courtyard is filled with poor and needy people to whom angels distribute gold, silver and also some loaves of bread, while two bishops worship before a chalice set on an altar placed in the centre of the painting. The icon is interesting, not only because of its unusual theme, the excellence of its linear rhythm and the beauty of its colours, but also because of its unusually sophisticated composition, the artist having chosen to give the assembled people a triangular grouping in order to carry the eye upwards, where a mural of the Virgin of the Sign and three traditional, onion-shaped golden domes direct not only the eye but also the mind towards heaven.

PLATE 48 THE GETHSEMANE Muscovite school of early to mid-eighteenth-century date. $8 \times 5\frac{1}{2}$ in. (20.3×13.9 cm.). Hann Collection, USA.

In iconography, this complex theme is represented by three scenes: that showing the agony in the garden, that of Christ waking the sleeping apostles, and that of Judas receiving the sum due to him for his betrayal. On the icon the first scene is given greatest prominence, for it occupies the centre of the panel, while that of Christ waking the apostles is shown below; Judas occupies a position to the left of the panel. Though the rendering of the rocks conforms to an early tradition, the work was carried out by a painter who no longer fully understood the convention, and who devoted much of the space on this small panel to showing, with considerable exactitude, an elaborate architectural building of late date. The foreshortening of the figures likewise points to a late date, and so too does the artist's attempt to present the three scenes, if not in perspective, at any rate on different planes. The faces of the chief priests come very close to portraiture, and the three scenes are rendered as a narrative rather than as a record of a deeply felt emotional experience. However, the colours are good, considerable stress being laid on the typically Russian shades of pink and deep green. Notwithstanding its late date the painting is in no way debased, and it serves to show that work of real competence continued to be produced by icon painters at a time when many of their fellow-artists had fully mastered the naturalistic styles of painting current in their day in western Europe.

I

2

3

4

5

6

8

9

10

11

12

13

14

16

17

18

19

20

22

23

24

25

27

28

30

31

33

34

35

Успение Пр͠стыѧ Б͠ци

36

37

38

40

41

ЖЕНЫ МИРОНОСИЦЫ ПРИИДОША КГРОБУ

42

44

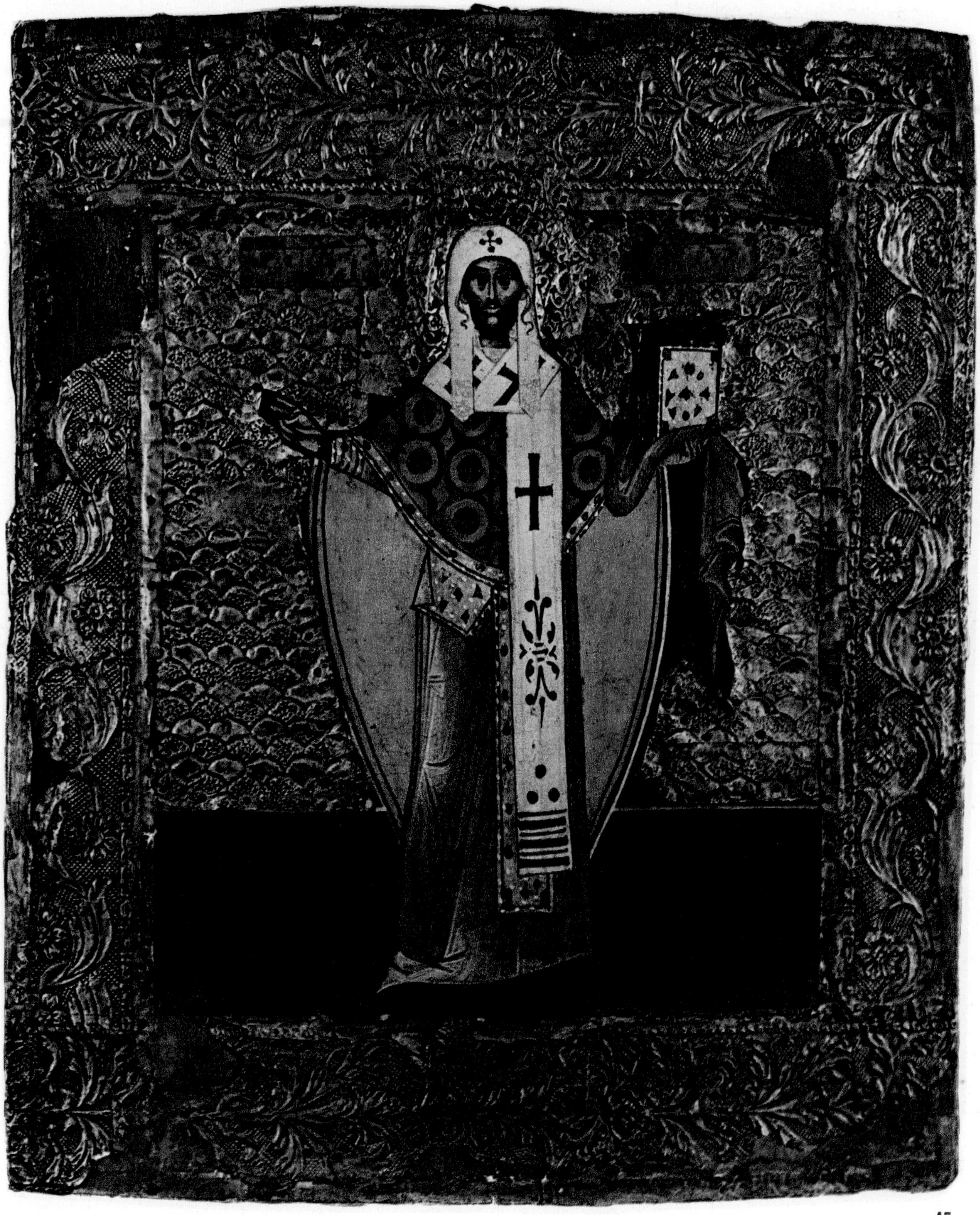

48